BEYOND THE BRANCH

Exploring the Hidden Life of the Stick Insect

MIKE PEARCE

DEDICATION

This book is dedicated to those who are interested in different aspects of stick insect biology and behaviour.

CONTENTS

Acknowledgments
Preview

1 The past   1

2 Habitat   3

3 Life history   4

4 Food   14

5 Biology and behaviour   18

6 Ways of defence   27

7 Masters of camouflage   33

8 Superstition and human resources   41

9 Pest status   43

10 Conclusion and useful bibliography   45

ACKNOWLEDGMENTS

The author would like to thank Christine Pearce
for reading and checking through the manuscript.

PREVIEW

Insects are the most successful and diverse of all invertebrates, stick insects certainly being one of them.

Stick insects, walking sticks, bug sticks, ghost insects, forest phantoms, wood nymphs, living twigs, as many call them are often thought of as drab, sluggish, often clumsy, clockwork, ugly insects, not known for their beauty as compared to say something like a jewel beetle.

Many know them from the Indian Stick insect popular with children. Within the three thousand plus herbivorous species there is a spectacular range of form, colour and behaviour.

This short book gives an overview of these attributes, illustrating the amazing diversity and adaptations especially camouflage, in the hope that readers may take the challenge to start studying and keeping such amazing and interesting insects as pets.

1 THE PAST

The unpredictable, spontaneous patterns seen in present day stick insects have been influenced by evolutionary selection based on environment and predator pressure which makes the insect changes seen complex and adaptive.

Stick insects were around 125 million years before flowering plants. They first appeared in the early Cretaceous and developed further characteristics in the Paleogene era. They are related to cockroaches, mantids and especially grasshoppers. Like other insects in the carboniferous many may have been very big. This was a time of extremes when oxygen levels were around 35 percent compared to 21 percent today. This meant that more oxygen was able to diffuse through their spiracles (breathing tubes) so that metabolism could be increased. Also, air density increased, and this benefited the evolution of aerial locomotion. It also is suggested that insects became so big e.g., seven-foot millipedes, so as to avoid the toxicity of excess oxygen if they were a smaller size.

Stick insects were around with dinosaurs and when the flowering plants became prominent 300 million years ago.

They were able to mimic plants or parts of plants helping them to avoid predators.

Various general names exist today for some stick insects such as children's, laboratory, charming, fast moving, Cyclone Larry, gecko, or false stick insect. Other names also exist which will be mentioned later in the text.

2 HABITAT

Stick insects are found all over the world except in the Antarctic. There are more in the tropics and subtropical environments. Some are found especially in Asia and South America. Many have specific humidity and temperature requirements. Lower temperatures and wet habitats in some tropical area encourages plant undergrowth which can ensure survival of eggs and development of young. Also, a few species can withstand cold temperatures in alpine regions. The presence of stick insects may be determined by tolerance not preference and they may survive in places where they don't prefer to exist but where there is least competition.

Many have been named after their origins such as the Florida, Vietnam. India, American stick insect.

3 LIFE HISTORY

Stick insects can breed the whole year round if they are in a hot climate. Some can become asexual if no male is present but if so, they may not adapt so quickly. One can also get gynandromorphs e.g., females with the wings of a male.

Pairs may copulate several times during the day. A preference may be for younger female insects. Some males can spend most of the time attached to the female, even all their lifespan, but not copulating. This can ensure fertilisation as well as providing protection.

 Females can release directional volatile chemicals at night so that males can find them. They can release more pheromones   than the male. Some insects can also smell like the host plants aiding recognition.

Sperm in some species can be injected into the body cavity of the female which increases the chances of reproduction whereas in others sperm is held in a spermatophore in a compartment near the tip of the abdomen. Less flight in females means more fecundity and the reduced need for aerial mobility in certain habitats. Some insects can produce two broods during spring and summer.

In large aggregations males can be aggressive, fighting for the females even biting antennae or legs of other males. Many males may lack a female in the non-mating season and in some cases the female can reproduce by pathogenesis not needing males. Their offspring are clones, all being females. Parthenogenicity is especially good if the female is restricted to one environment, the environment is unsuitable, or they need to recolonise new habitats and reproduce more quickly. Eggs from parthenogenetic insects take longer to hatch.

Eggs

Eggs may be laid either night or day or both day and night. Laying may be linked to light and dark cycles. Sizes of eggs vary greatly from two millimetres to over one centimetre in length. The larger the insect the bigger the egg can be. If big there is also possibly less need for camouflage or elaboration of the egg surface. In temperate regions egg laying is seasonal often the eggs overwintering and dormant the adults dying off. Some eggs can even overwinter for several seasons.

Numbers of eggs produced by stick insects can exceed thousands in their lifetime. Some can produce over eighty in a week whereas others can produce only one egg a day.

Where large numbers of eggs are produced there is often high mortality both of eggs and nymphs and as breeders also know not all eggs will hatch.

The extraordinary variety of stick insect eggs provide an insight into the diversity of life on earth. Many eggs resemble the seeds of plants. You just have to see the seeds of the castor oil plants (Ricinus) and passion fruit to see the resemblance. Different shapes, surfaces, sizes and sculptured features can be species specific.

Stick insects can either glue eggs to leaves or twigs or skewer leaves. Many other eggs are just dropped, buried or pushed into soil or crevices. Eggs need to be camouflaged, blending in with their surroundings and tend to be in some cases hardened brown or black, or with a sticky surface. Small eggs may be influenced by the presence of water, surface tension sticking them to the leaf or one another. Eggs in dry conditions can take longer to hatch and may not do so. Insects can lose water through egg production so need to have a water source available.

Smaller eggs like seeds tend to have a quicker germination/hatching time. Large seeds/eggs need longer juvenile periods. Some eggs have a waxy outer coating or may be covered in calcium oxalate insoluble crystals obtained from the plants or other toxic substances which can cause irritation to predators if eaten.

On one side of all eggs is a micropyle at the end or middle of a flattened, often paler coloured area the micropylar plate. This micropylar pore is often raised up with a lip and its purpose is for fertilisation. With parthenogenetic insects there is no need for fertilisation. Here all offspring produced will be females or with a rare exception a male. Wingless, or those with reduced wings can produce more eggs. Stick insects only have one sex chromosome X Females are therefore XX. If one accidentally loses a chromosome XO one can get a male.

Eggs need moisture and humidity to develop. The surface of eggs may have pores over the surface allowing entry of water and gases to aid development. Some eggs may become mouldy but still hatch. Larger or flatter eggs may be more prone to predation, but you would need a lot of eggs to make a worthwhile meal for large predator.

It is believed by some that eggs were transported to other regions of the world on sea water as floating eggs or within floating plants. Coconut stick insect eggs can survive in sea water for over a year. Today they can be transported in soil and imported plants. It has also been found that where female stick insects containing eggs with hardened shells have been eaten by some bird species these eggs can pass through the bird's gut as seeds do and still hatch afterwards.

The Buriers

 Here the female can make a hole in the soil and insert the egg, raising its abdomen over its head to do so. It can then flick soil on top. Some can lay several eggs in a pit. Burying eggs may make them be more exposed to parasites than those laid higher up in trees. But if they are buried there is less need for camouflage. They can be laid vertical or flat sometimes together with faeces or ingested soil and can be buried as deep as six centimetres. Some eggs may only hatch if covered with soil by the female and it is said soil covering or burying helps them withstand bush fires.

Droppers or flickers

Successful dropping depends on the shape or weight of the egg. These insects tend to lay more eggs than with other methods. The abdomen is straightened and flicked forward. Dropping eggs from great heights can sound like rain falling. Indian stick insects can drop eggs at random during the day at rest or whilst feeding during the night.

Many eggs are spherical so readily roll off leaves and fall to the ground, into crevices or leaf axils. Many have a small often white or yellowish umbrella or mushroom shaped protrusion (the elaiosome) at one end. This is attached centrally in the opercular lid (capitulum) which may be perforated.at the end at which they will emerge. The capitulum may also absorb water. The elaiosome is thought possibly to contain fats or sugars attractive to ants and in some species the eggs are carried into their nests where the stick insects hatch and later escape from dump sites. The hatched insects themselves look like ants so are able to escape without being attacked.

Some eggs from stick insects are flicked away from the faecal droppings many centimetres away so that predators are not attracted. Generalists can drop eggs anywhere, while specialist plant feeders stick to laying them on or close to these plants so that the offspring don't have to search for specific plants.

Some eggs are flattened and maybe carried in the wind, float to the ground, or maybe become stuck to leaves by surface tension. Other eggs can be conical shaped so roll in a tight circle on a leaf surface like some bird's eggs that prevents them from falling off cliffs.

The clingers

Some stick insects' eggs are covered in hairy or fringed protrusions, some to a great extent. Often these protrusions may be closely packed and glued together with sticky brown residue which dissolves away in high humidity or water such as rain. Protrusions can even be cemented together with wax.

Their stickiness may help them adhere to animals' fur or feathers or even other insects. Other protruding forms such as hairs or bristles on some eggs may also have the same function. Not all eggs with protrusions are left exposed. Some with hairy hooks are buried. Some flickers with hairy eggs bury them, the eggs being flicked over the abdomen which may even have a male on top and the eggs positioned by the antennae and front legs. It is suggested as these eggs have hooked hairs these are captured by the hairy antennae when flicked.

Gluers and piercers

Here the female can produce an adhesive liquid from the end of her abdomen to glue the eggs on top or the underside of leaves. Some eggs are elongated with hardened pointed ends and spines and inserted into leaves or crevices. They may even have a skirt near the end of the egg ensuring the eggs stand upright on the leaf. Rows of barbs on their surface can ensure they stay put, anchoring the egg so that it does not move when the insect emerges. Eggs are often laid together in the same place, sometimes in clutches or rows. One stick insect is known to produce an ootheca full of eggs similar to mantids.

Hatching

Time before hatching can vary between three to eighteen months depending on temperature. With large insects and parthenogenetic one's egg hatching can be longer. However the Indian stick insect hatching time can be as short as two to four months.

Hatching can occur alternate years some overwintering for two years. e.g., in the Rocky Mountains. Hatching is usually at night and can occur in the rainy season with humidity high and moisture acting as a lubricant. Nymphs on emerging are often hyperactive and climb upwards towards the light, which they seem to be attracted to. There is safety at the top and also new leaves which may have a higher sugar content.

It seems extraordinary that a hatched insect can be as much as eight times the size of the egg it has emerged from. Some species especially have very long spindly legs. Inside the egg the nymph is coiled, its head, tail and legs are curved forwards then backwards. The first pair of legs can be folded on itself four times. The head is right against the exit lid. It straightens out its body which may help flip off the lid. The head emerges first, then the thorax is pulled out and abdomen, followed by the antennae, front, middle and finally back legs. The insects can use their legs to push the egg off them, or drag the egg along a leaf or try to shake it off. After hatching the nymphs inflate themselves to become larger.

Ecdysis

Moulting can occur 4-10 times and the female can have one extra moult compared to the male. The process is similar to hatching. It can occur at a certain time of day especially when predators less abundant.. Just before moulting the body becomes distended. It stops eating and has lost most of its gut contents.. It does not breathe during moulting.

The insect hangs upside down from its hind legs, the tarsal patches being extremely adhesive. The body arches at the prothorax. Blood enters the soft membrane joining the head to the thorax and the pouch produced projects behind the head, The insect swallows air to pump up its body, and the old skin starts to split longitudinally. This split gradually increases in length and it then pushes its prothorax out. First the head emerges, then the thorax then the abdomen. Middle legs are first, then the antennae, then front and hind legs but this can vary. It then can flip around and proceed to eat its moult at this site or on the ground if it is dropped. All the moulted bits including the tarsi can be eaten.

At the last moult some insects, especially males can become another colour e.g., reds or blues. Brown coloured females can become bright green. Moulting can be a time where malformations can occur. Noise or movement can affect moulting. Sometimes legs can be formed at an odd angle, but it does not affect their health.

Longevity

Adults stick insects can usually live six months to a year. Males often do not live as long as females but can mature faster. Some like the jungle nymphs, the second heaviest insects after beetles, can live for two years. Slender insects are more fragile. Some stick insects live with others and tend to be passive. A Frankenstein like report has related that cutting the head of an insect and then replacing it will rejoin except for the nervous chord.

Some insects without food can survive for several days, the larger ones living longer.

4 FOOD

Many stick insects have coevolved with plants, some still feed on conifers and ferns. Most stick insects can survive on the Rosacea family which includes bramble.

Stick insects are found feeding in tropical, temperate forests, grasslands or dry regions, their food being the leaves of trees and shrubs. They can be found in gardens, parks and agricultural land. Some may remain during the day under bark or boards on the ground or resting on walls or houses.and return to their food source at night. The presence of phasmids are a good indicator of good health, the wider the variety, the wider the variety of plant. Where some are restricted only to a few hectares and there is a need to encourage conservation.

Stick insect jaws are faced forward and they use two claws and four suction pads on their feet, to cling to vegetation. Sticky pads may vary in form and there can be more sticky pads on long legged insects. Smell can be important in some cases in their search for food and some insects may have more olfactory proteins i.e. a greater sense of smell.

The age of a leaf can be linked to the degree of feeding.

Some adults may prefer older foliage, even very old. However, fresh leaves can be toxic especially to nymphs e.g. where oils or astringent tannins are at higher levels e.g., eucalyptus. Toxicity can also build up with constant feeding and kills, as is sometimes seen when feeding on ivy.

Stick insects can be host specific. These specialist feeders are more resistant to toxins in younger leaves. In S.W USA they can feed on creosote bushes. Non specialist feeders are able to pick and choose and may have a wider tolerance to these plant chemicals. This is useful where they have to switch to a new food plant when the original is not available. The Indian stick insect is a fairly non-specialist feeder and unlike many other stick insects can eat a large range of food types.

Many insects feed at night, a time when it is safer from predators, but some feed in the day. Many exhibit negative geotaxis so move upwards during the night where fresher leaves are available. Nymphs when hatched can move upwards to where there is increased light.

In captivity if no other food is available some breeders say they can feed stick insects on the green part of lettuce, broccoli, carrots, cauliflower, kale, even skinned cucumber, apples and other fruits. However, insects feeding on a particular food source may be accustomed to it and may not accept alternatives. Some also may abandon their preferred food source where there is a seasonal change in leaf composition. Altering the food source can affect the preference of the next generation e.g., moving from bramble to ivy may make the new generation prefer ivy. Stems of plants can be eaten as well as the harder surface tissue of hard stems. Compounds in the foods eaten may provide insect distastefulness for any predator trying to eat them.

Larger insects as expected can have big appetites when feeding. All insects can make semicircular cuts in leaves eating in an up and down movement like a caterpillar then returning to where they started. Many can eat through tough leaves like palms.

The muscular proventriculus inside the stick insect gut has spines. Here leaves are shredded into smaller pieces to be attacked by digestive enzymes in the midgut. Cellulases and pectinases can break down cells and cell walls to glucose. There appears to be no gut enlargements for bacterial fermentation but some may though have microbes to reduce toxins. The anterior part of the midgut is acid while post midgut is more alkaline. It is suggested that filaments in the posterior end of the midgut are involved with excretory or secretory functions. The faeces contain uric acid often with dark green and white spots. They can be wet, black and elongated or may be as dry pellets, water being reabsorbed from rectal contents. Non plant material may also be found in the faeces even aluminium foil if present in a culture can be eaten.

In overcrowded situations where there is a lack of food there may be cannibalism. Sometimes legs are accidentally eaten. Larger insects are known to eat weaker ones. Stick insects will also eat their own or other moults providing a source of protein. Plants provide moisture. But many insects tend to drink available moisture from rain etc. If thirsty they will move their mouth parts over surfaces searching for moisture. Where excess water is present Insects can totally submerge their heads in water to drink as they don't breathe through their mouths.

5 BIOLOGY AND BEHAVIOUR

Body shape

Insects may be as short as a few centimetres in length, while others can manage to reach sixty-four centimetres with extended legs. But being this long makes vertical climbing a challenge as well as avoiding being visible to predators. Many of these long insects exist high up in the tree canopy.

Stick insects can be thin with long spindly legs or can be robust, more solid looking. Bodies are mainly green or brown close to the colour of plant stems and leaves. They also can be flattened, while others more rounded twig like and even may have a bend in them. Many have the longest antennae in the insect world. Some have different head shapes with the top extended backwards by elongated swellings.

General names to illustrate body size or shape include, great thin, chocolate log, cigar, short horned, twisted, short rumped slender bodied, humpback, bamboo noded and thick thighed stick insect.

Many females, unlike males, may not fly and are often

sedentary being restricted to an environment or food source. Females can become huge in size reaching over sixty grams. Being big and fat egg laying machines means that they can often fall off plants.

This large size has given rise to several names such as megabeast, giant, gargantuan, titan, goliath, tree lobster, walking sausage and policeman's truncheon stick insects.

Movement

Activity varies, some insects being more active than others. Nymphs are often more hyperactive especially after hatching. Mobility in many older insects is not great, and some get so fat they hardly move and may not move hind legs much. Moving slowly though does have an advantage being less attractive to predators. Darkness can trigger activity.

When walking not more than three feet are raised at any one time. The hind legs provide the energy to move forward the middle for braking and steering. If middle legs are lost there is four step motion. Some walk slowly, stop and remain motionless. Often long-legged insects can become entangled together. There is also a lot of swaying to and fro when walking for these insects or when disturbed. Insects are more active during windy days and sway mimicking moving leaves by bending their tarsal and knee joints.

Insects can support themselves hanging down on one leg illustrating the great adhesiveness of tarsal pads. Some walk or leap away if disturbed or can even kick and jump like a locust. Very active insects tend to have a shorter lifespan. On stems insects can arch their bodies backwards. Sense organs all over the body respond to touch and temperature. Mated females can be aggressive towards other females or males shaking or beating their legs on the substrate.

Antennae

Antennae are long and thin and bendable and may taper at the end. They can have 8-10 segments depending on the species. These can be as long as 165mm in a female and 115mm in a male and can vary in thickness. Some antennae are the same length as legs. Those insects with long antenna use them for tactile sampling. They move them and front legs in a rhythmical movement in a series of loops in front of them until they contact an object. This is especially important at night where their eyes are used less. As well as tactile cues antennae also have chemical, olfactory and hygro receptors. Smell can inhibit locomotion. They also have Johnston's organ sensory cells on the pedicel which can detect vibrations/sound waves as well as other and sensitive cells at the base of antennae.

Where antennae are small, legs can perform in a similar way. If antennae are lost legs take over forward waving and circling. The second pair of legs also can be used if first legs are lost.

Rhymical contractions in the dorsal blood vessel in stick insects may not allow haemolymph to reach the longer appendages, including the antennae. Small heart like structures behind the brain, attached to the frontal cuticle close to the base of the antennae can help pump in haemolymph to the antennae.

Sensitivity

Sound

Stick insects can distinguish between predator and noise. Some adults can rub legs together to produce low clicking noise all at the same time. Stretch receptors may be adapted for sound detection on antennae and forelegs, mouth parts and abdomen. Two chordotonal organs on the proximal tibia can detect vibrations being most sensitive above 800 HZ. The cerci may also be able to pick up vibrations. Some say stick insects respond to playing the piano.

Temperature

It is suggested that for most insects 25 degrees centigrade is the optimum but normally 17-25 degrees centigrade is a perfect range. Warmer night temperatures can increase metabolism, feeding activity and growth. Thermoreceptor cells are all over the body as well as on the antennae. Matt black insects can have higher heat absorption.

However, in the tropics the temperature at night can go down to 10 degrees centigrade. Also, in New Zealand alpine regions or the Andes, Central Chile, temperatures are close to 0 degrees centigrade. Some insects can survive these lower temperatures becoming disorientated, lethargic and dormant. They may have trehalose and glucose used as an antifreeze in their blood.

Some stick insects may over winter in other places, often moving to areas where they can bask in the sunshine. Those found in colder districts are possibly unable to fly. Many insects die off in winter leaving their eggs to hatch as the temperature increases. Cold temperatures can delay egg development. Some eggs can survive temperatures of minus 5 degrees centigrade or several long periods of sharp frosts. Temperature can also affect the sex of eggs. If high, one may get partial male characters on female insects. Stick insects will try to move away from high temperatures including grass fires. Temperatures thirty degrees centigrade and above can be detrimental. In sunlight some insects move into shade or can even slide down into leaf bases to avoid heat.

Vision

A bright light may cause stick insects to move their head side to side. A moving light can stop insect movement. There seems no response to red light, but they are attracted to lamps at night like the moon light.

Nymphs are attracted to light and move upwards. As the insect grows the number of facets and photocells in the eye increase. Larger eyes are more sensitive to radiation, so adults are mainly nocturnal. Photoreceptor density is low so they possibly only see courser details It is reported that some insets do not see colour but where they do, they could have UV, blue and green sensitive photoreceptors. Some brightly coloured stick insects may have evolved with visual systems.

Some compound eyes have a black spot in the centre, the pseudopupil. Here these facets reflect less being directly inline facing the viewer than other facets. Each eye has multiple lenses and no single lens. Motion detecting cells are in the insect's optic lobe. Stick insects can discriminate between ventral and horizontal shapes. Rocking may also help sort out objects. In the day younger nymphs are active but they are less nocturnally adapted than adults, so vision is less good in dim light while the adults have a greater sensitivity at night

Many variations in eye colour are seen in stick insects. Some can have yellow eyes with vertical stripes on, chestnut brown eyes with cream patches in lines, green eyes with a brown line straight across the centre, cream eyes with purple circles in rings and stripes, and even green eyes with purple parallel lines from top to bottom to mention a few. The presence of pigmented patterns in the eyes could possibly increase with age. The coloured pigmented patterns could make images less sharp, more diffuse but able to perceive movement, bright light being avoided causing them to move into vegetation. Those insects with no pigmentation patterns may see better sharply defined images in bright sunlight and possibly mean individuals may stay together.

Between the compound eyes some insects can have three ocelli in a triangle. These can register brightness, but not direction and may help adjust the sensitivity of the compound eyes. They respond to light more than darkness. Some insects may have only one or two ocelli.

Those having ocelli are likely from past winged ancestors. There is a high probability that if the insect is a flier, it will have ocelli. Winged insects can be attracted to UV and white light. Some can fly around room lights and even avoid obstacles.

Grouping

Young insects tend to cluster. Fourth instar insects can clump or form chains attached to one another on food plants. Some young and adult insects and especially non-spiny insects can also group together as stick forms forming a tight bunch.

Some stick insects can remain on the ground during the day. They may rest under objects, bitten off leaves, bark or stones. At night they leave and return to where they live in the day. Adults and nymphs in these groups can pile on top of each other as adults but with spines cannot curl up. If on the ground bodies may be close to the ground heads pointing the same way. Being on the ground will expose them to predators. It is suggested that nymphs can group around female to defend her. It is even suggested, within these closely bound groups social hierarchies and social and antagonistic behaviour may exist, an alpha insect possibly leading the group. Possibly like locusts one can also get solitary or gregarious forms. In larger densities the body colour changes green to black or brown. On vegetation one may get two different species living close together without conflict. However, if the food resource runs out or there is overpopulation one can get cannibalisation, the weaker and small more vulnerable ones often being eaten.

6 WAYS OF DEFENCE

The Red Queen Hypothesis states that in order to survive both predator and prey must evolve with each other. With the use of camouflage predators have to waste time searching for these insects.

Predators of stick insects include birds, ants, reptiles, spiders, wasps, bats, rats, centipedes, millipedes and mantises. Primates and small mammals can also eat them. Larger stick insects are not prey to spiders and mantids. Bird colour vison is not uniform and can be impaired depending on light intensity and background colouration. Most birds can see red, yellow, orange and green clearly but not blue very well and violet not at all. Insects are hard to see at a distance especially if they have a stick like appearance. To ensure predators don't associate insect droppings, some stick insects shoot their droppings a few metres away.

Thanatosis (Playing dead).

Some insects' front legs fit perfectly at the side of their heads when stretched forward with the antennae. If disturbed, they can drop like sticks to the ground and remain in this position for several hours. This is a cataleptic response; the insect can appear dead for long periods of time. Tapping their body or holding them upside down between second and third legs can freeze them. Slow flexor and tensor neurons in muscles fire at the same time in thanatosis. They can be brought back to life by gentle pressure 2cm from the end of the abdomen or if held upside down righted. Recovery is instant in all cases. Some insects if large may do this, fall to the ground, then run away. Some may jump backwards and fall to the ground. Others non stick like insects can remain frozen in situ, and remain motionless

Rocking

Stick insects may rock in situ or when walking. The tail is often also curled upwards. This rocking also often occurs in windy conditions so that they do not stand out when leaves are moving at the same time. It can be more intense in areas with high winds. Rocking may also have other significances. Large groups of young insects in cages with no draughts have been seen to rock side to side swaying in unison for up to thirty minutes starting and stopping for no reason. A similar situation was seen just before sunset.

Regeneration

Some insects can readily lose a leg at the coxal trochanteral joint if attacked. Some are so fragile that can lose several legs. This can stimulate regeneration causing it to moult. Replacement is under a black cap often with a small hook-like leg reduced in size which is remedied and workable after several moults. Legs may not be replaced if nearer the trochanter. If they have reached the last moult legs cannot regenerate. If an insect loses its antennae this cannot be replaced but on occasions a small leg will appear in its place. The loss of legs may be related in the past to loss of wings. Where haemolymph is lost wounds can close after a few hours.

Spines

One can get an idea about the reputation of those stick insects with spines or thorny extensions. by the common names given to them - great spiny, giant prickly, thorny devil, warty, devils darning needle, gnarled twig, rough prairie alligator, McCauley's spectre, spiny head, black spined, touch me not, jungle dragon, bristly, spiny ridge backed and spur legged stick insects.

With each moult the spines can become larger. Spines or protrusions are seen on heads, legs, thorax or all over the body surface. Some protrusions are even multispined projections or antler like. Those insects that look more like sticks tend to have few, if any, spines. There are fewer spines on younger insects while larger insects have more developed spines, some very big especially on legs or thorax. The female though may have more spines overall. Long and short spines can be found some along and at the sides of the thorax some bodies are completely covered with short spines. Some spines may be as horns on the head.

Spines can be curved or straight, arranged singly, in rows, pairs or groups. Several have rows of spines on the femur or a big, large spine often more developed in the male. They can strike out with their legs to grab or injure a disturber. Fore legs may have rows of spines acting as a saw-like blade.

Spines can also be brightly coloured e.g., red or orange often matching different parts of the body. Spines are reduced where there are wings. Those insects that curve their abdomen upwards to mimic scorpions can have numerous spines on their underside exposed as adults.

Not all stick insects have spines such as the unarmed stick insect. Some insects can depend on the spines of plants along the edge of leaves for protection The insect's legs in line with the body sit in the grooves or furrows in the midribs during the day and feed at night.

Chemical

Some insects may have volatile or toxic secretions derived from the oils and other chemicals such as terpenes found in some plants Two sac like glands in metathorax behind the head can emit toxic burning secretions These can be shot out as a fine spray at predators or competing males as far as thirty centimetres often several times. This ability can occur after hatching or the first moult and winged insects can have this form of defence. Others can produce tear gas like volatile chemicals with repulsive and corrosive effects. Many chemicals have a characteristic smell such as peppermint or toffee.

Another chemical defence includes the distasteful foul-smelling green, yellow haemolymph derived from blue pigments and carotenoids that can be released from joints or inside the insect itself. Other insects may regurgitate their white or yellowish sticky stomach contents, blow bubbles or even emit a vapour from the rear end of their abdomen as small puffs producing a cracking sound.

These forms of defence have given rise to names such as spitting devil, musk mare, witches horse, dragon, devils riding horse. The name mule killer refers to the possible poisoning of horses which ate these insects.

7 MASTERS OF CAMOUFLAGE

Nature's adaptive experiments frustrate recognition and identity. But once movement occurs any cryptic devises become ineffectual. Where the cryptic form is lost this can trigger increased predation on stick insects and other insects as well, this can seriously affect the stability of an environment.

Common names illustrating forms of camouflage and defence include black beauty, brown beauty, green bean, jewelled, blue, peppermint, painted, lime green, blue green, red and black, red, moss, green jewel, two striped, three striped, red striped, green striped, lichen, moss, white, white kneed, orange kneed, yellow spotted, rose winged, metallic and Peruvian fire stick insect.

Form resemblance

As mentioned previously stick insect eggs can resemble seeds and may be attractive to insects such as ants. In some stick insects the first pair of legs fit around the head. The femora fit closely to the head and when stretched out parallel to the outstretched antennae give the full stick effect. Insects can also jut out at a similar angle to twigs and some even can bend their bodies to do so. Limbs can appear like leaf veins or expanded like foliage. Body segments can mimic the distance between nodes on twigs. Spines similar to the food plant fed on may help concealment, but if too many then can't do stick pose as they can't fold up. Protrusions as in insects looking like lichens, moss, dead crumpled leaves or rough pimpled surfaces can also help concealment. Keeping giant prickly stick insect first instar nymphs with lichens can produce a lichen effect but this can revert back to green as adult. Some insects also rock when the wind moves the leaves so as not to stand out.

Colour resemblance (Background)

As mentioned previously stick insect eggs with their various patterns and sculpturing can be camouflaged with the surroundings on the ground. The young when hatched are often better camouflaged than the adult insects. Some insects can become lighter after hatching on the ground and moving into vegetation.

Many stick insects are brown or green similar to twigs and leaves. Colours include pea and other shades of green, chocolate brown, orange brown and all black. They can become paler or darker with age or through an optical stimulus response to their surroundings causing movement of pigment in epidermal cells. They also can be darker at night or with greater humidities. On top or underside leaves they may match colours, white insects matching the underside. Some insects can change from green to straw to brown. Females tend to blend in more than males and males can be greener than females so move more in leaves. Some insects have bright smudge like colours along their body length. which match lichens on branches. Others may have moss or lichens growing on their bodies. Some change colour after the last nymphal stage such as brown to green. There can be polymorphism, different forms of the same species and colour can also be different for those insects that have been produced sexually or asexually.

Depending on the predator's vision acuity some may not see them against the background, but others can discriminate.

Obliterative

Here counter lighting and darkening, can delete a roundish appearance, destroy depth and three-dimensional space. This is seen on stick insect legs especially but also on antennae. The legs can have along their length small or extended stripes of another colour they may have semicircles of different colour or rectangles along their edges or smudges along their length. Legs can also have coloured joints e.g., black legs with red or orange joints,

Some insects can have spots of colour over them or speckles or mottling. Males may be less mottled. Dazzle patterns of yellow, whites or greens even blue have an effect. White patches can look like bird droppings. Some colours together can appear grey at a distance a fact which was utilised for disguise during world wars.

Disrupting colourations

Contrasting colours or tones blur the outline and lose form and destroys quick recognition. Patches of contrasting colours draw attention away from shape. Where two colours are adjacent a dark dividing line between the two colours can increase effectiveness. If colours are at the edges of the body, they can break up form especially if they match their background. There are numerous examples of contrasting colour patches. Yellow on black insects, white on brown, orange on green and blue on brown for example.

Many stick insects can have stripes of a contrasting colour along the top of their bodies or sides. These may be as light markings on dark or dark markings on light. These stripes can be from head to tail, thorax to tail broken striped or as coloured triangles along the length. White marks on dark insects used sparingly are best with the very light and deepest shades next to one another. Like snakes they break up elongated forms. Some insects may have two stripes breaking up their appearance. Colours can include white and orange stripes on a brown or black body, yellow stripes on black or green insects, black stripes on red, to mention a few. Elongated stripes are especially effective on plants with needle shaped leaves. There also may be stripes across the body e.g., a green body with yellow or black stripes across the segments. Dark brown or black stripes can merge in with darker shadows while black and white diagonal lines can break up sharp angles.

Complex shapes

Different tones can exist with removal of cast shadows by modifying orientation. Some insects can be darker on top than beneath so that the upper side does not look brighter in light.

Closeness to stems or pressing bodies right against twigs or trunks can reduce shadow. as can being beneath a leaf or stalk moving in the breeze. Tucking in limbs will reduce shadow. Serrations or fringes can also remove shadows e.g., lichen like insects. Some stick insects can form a ball if threatened, the legs being placed under the thorax the abdomen going over the thorax to the head.

Advertisement

Some stick insects appear to have avoided camouflage and display bright colours on their bodies and legs as spots and stripes or total colour. Colours can include bright red, deep red, ultramarine and green, red, blue and yellow and bright white. It is an evolutionary lottery. The bright ones may be small in number, but they survive, spread through populations and more may be selected. There are always different ways of doing things.

These colourful insects may act as beacons of distastefulness to predators often having chemical defence mechanisms as secretions or in their bodies, possibly derived from toxic plants. e.g., fern eaters can have to deal with the fern's cyanide contents. Distasteful advertising can cause the predator to remember the colour that gave it trouble before.

Bright warning colours may only be useful in a single region where predators have learnt the signals. Some insects may have bright patches on their bodies. Many of the bright colours are only seen in the males, some of which are active in the day but are still partially camouflaged. The bright colours though may be attractive to females. Red or bright yellow on black is prominent for distasteful purposes. The sudden rapid sight of black, white, orange, yellow spots or bars or stripes can startle or terrify.

Startle response

Some insects have short elytra and wings. These can be long or miniature and are usually coloured. Wings are often only seen in the males which fly or glide down when in stress and some may not have spiny legs. Wings and wing buds increase in size with moult. Reduced forewings can conceal the large folded hindwings which are then flashed out to startle the predator

They can raise their wings and withdraw them or raise them open for many seconds startling the predator who will withdraw. Some wings can also make a rustling sound when opening or a swooshing sound by rubbing wings adding to the effect. It can be quite a frightening sight to see a stick insect with wings spread out front legs pointing forwards and its abdomen curved forwards and moving in a stabbing movement like a scorpion.

Spots may be on the wings or wings can be coloured. Examples include black or ultramarine insects with small red wings, brown insects with black wings with light brown patches or with transparent venated, mosaic dragonfly like wings, green insects with pink wings, green or yellow insects with orange wings and black semicircles or triangles to mention a few.

8 SUPERSTITION AND HUMAN RESOURCE

Stick insect eggs have been boiled and eaten in Borneo and Sarawak. The insects themselves have been roasted like locusts when abundant. Those with large spines on the male's femora legs have been used as fishhooks in D'entre Casteaux Islands near New Guinea. In Papua.New Guinea the chemical spray of stick insects can be used to treat skin infections. Stick insects are used in some countries as medicine for diarrhoea and mixed with herbs for ointment.

In China they may be kept in cages like crickets as tokens of good fortune. Stick insects are one of the twelve items in the Chinese zodiac for longevity and good health.

If an insect is found inside a house in Malaysia it can mean good luck. While in New Zealand the Māori believed if one fell onto you, you would be in a sacred site. Also in New Zealand if one fell onto a woman, she would be pregnant, and depending on the species this would determine the sex of the child. Seeing a stick insect in a drought could also indicate rain is coming.

In West Indian folk law, it is said that God rides place to

place on walking sticks. Various societies and religions worldwide see the stick insects as an example of change and transformation. Shedding skin represents death and rebirth. ˙On the other hand, stick insects can be seen linked to camouflage and deception.

Stick insects' eggs have been taken up to space aboard space shuttles including apollo 17 to see the effect of ionic radiation. Results indicated a possible   shorter lifespan and high rate of deformity.

9 PEST STATUS

With increased fecundity of females, especially for parthenogenetic ones, numbers can increase dramatically. One can get periodic outbreaks and thousands of eggs laid, which can devastate vegetation and crops. A sudden rise in temperature in spring can initiate massive hatchings of eggs. One observer when walking through a heavily infested wooded area said he could hear the eggs falling to the ground like hail. There are several records where stick insects have stripped leaves of orchards or partially defoliated trees. Stick insects can be wasteful feeders only partially eating leaves causing them to die or fall. Some species can attack and skeletonise leaves of cocoa, orange, oil palm, guava, and trees in parks such as oaks and limes e.g., in New Zealand the ring barker phasmid.

After attack in one area, stick insects may move to another site. Winged insects can parachute down into new areas and climb up other plants. Roads can form barriers often more to females who are heavier or may not fly. Situations occur where there are so many, they can crowd on one another, cover fences and even people. High populations in some areas can increase predation while leaving other areas abandoned to predators populations could blossom the next year. In Fiji and Samoa stick insects can strip coconut fronds leaving only the mid-ribs and can kill hundreds of trees. They live on the underside of older fronds on older trees. Older control methods included burning fronds so that the smoke caused them to drop off and be eaten by chickens. Populations can be monitored by using the density of frass dropped on the ground or even smoke to bring them down from trees.

Some stick insects are specific to small restrictive areas of the world. It is important to conserve these habitats as well as maintain the food plant present especially if these insects are specialist feeders.

10 CONCLUSION AND USEFUL BIBLIOGRAPHY

The hidden world of stick insects provides an insight into the creative world of nature's ingenuity both in camouflage and behaviour. Although stick insects may seem to some to be rather drab, clumsy insects many can be spectacularly beautiful especially those with wings. There are still many new species to find and stick insects will always remain important insects for study as well as providing easy to maintain pets.

Useful Bibliograhy

Baxter R. N. 2002 Rearing Stick and Leaf Insects Chudleigh Publishing

Brock.P.D.1999 The Amazing World of stick and Leaf Insects Amateur Entomologist Volume 26

Brock P.D. 2003 Rearing and Studying Leaf Insects Amateur Entomologist Volume 22

Clark. J.T. 1974 Stick and Leaf Insects Redwood Burn Ltd

Floyd.D.2007 Keeping Stick insects. Deanprint Ltd

Other publications by the include videos on youtube- The Wow Factor of Stick Insect Eggs and Stick Insect Accommodation. Also many of the aspects mentioned in this book can be found in The Stick Insect behaviour series also online.

To see other publications below by the author visit **snappysnappybooks.com or just search Dr Mike Pearce Amazon books.**

Many of these books in these volumes are also published individually

SNAPPY SNAPPY COLLECTIONS:

Volume 1. BUSINESS AND SELF CONFIDENCE

How to be a Successful Business Weed
Clingers, Creepers and Scramblers
How to Deal with Life's Snakes and Ladders
Trust-Nothing but a Must
Know Your Students and Build Your Image
Hidden from the Heart but not Forgotten
More Pens for Pops
Charity Shops

Volume 2. IDENTITIES, HANG UPS AND CONCERNS

I Herring Gull
Pulvi Royal
I am Termite
Go Fat Go

Make up-Revealed
Fertility Stones and Chocolate Eggs
Captain Grottbuster versus the Grey World
The kittiwakes Warning
Wastefulness-Bone and Urine
Tails, Tales
A slice of Slang with a touch of Cockney and a drop
of Dorset
Mr Hamstrings Dinner

Volume 3. HORROR AND HISTORY

The Living Fossils
My Therizinosaurus
Human Termites eat London
Pigeons Splat London
Glass Anemones Tentacle-ize London
Beware of Cucumbers, Apples and Pigs
The Cornish Urchin
Baby Toes
Googolplex of Mice
Screaming Alley
The Night Mare
Queen Rat on Deadman's Island
Dead Donkey Lane
Old Mother Nature laughed and Laughed
The Plaster Room

Volume 4. RELIGION AND HOPEFULNESS

Pattern for Purpose God's and Man's designs
The Littlest Oyster

Tuppeny Hangover
In a Dark, Dark Corner was the Holy Ghost
The Little Shepherd Boy's Gift
Spider in the Tomb
The Sparrows' Last Soul
The Pawnbroker's Souls
The Red Church Doll
The Boy who found Christmas
The Eggstraordinary Easter Egg
Little Mary
Shepherd's Purse
Sitting next to Angels
The White Lily-St Mildred-Patron Saint of Thanet

Volume 5. TIDE AND TIME

The Shell Man
The Shell Lady
The Watcher on the Fal
The Rock Pool
A Call under the Sea
Pocket full of Starfish
The Scrofula Infirmary
Till my Lips were Salt as Brine
The Man with a Book on his Head
Coloured Bricks
The Girl Under the Paeony Tree
Nothing but Leaves
The China Blackbird
The Man who Collected Figures
The Rusty Gate
Time Runs Dry (a play set in a care home)

Volume 6. FAIRY TALES AND POEMS

The Nursery Rhyme Cat
 Cats at Christmas

The Tuppeny Bear
The Giant and the Giraffe Boy
The Giant's Toothpick
The White Cockerel
The Old Pot and the Golden Shoes
Ball Rooms
Exodus to a Leaf
The Forlorn Fruit Fly
Two Sleepy Boys
Mrs Light and Mr Dark
 I'm Just Going to the Bathroom
The Tulip Tree
The Man who always Sprinted
Bits and Bobs (Poems and short stories for children)

Volume 7. A VARIETY OF WOMEN

Photosynthetic Women
Absorbed by a Woman
The Slothful Wife
Betty's Barcodes
Valentines Cards
The Lady loves Red

The Woman who Smelled Books
Boy, Could She Smell!
The Lady who loved Hairspray

Volume 8. CHRISTMAS BOOKS

Impy Christmas
The Little Shepherd Boys Gift
The Boy who found Christmas
Oh, father Christmas what yer going to do?
Nothing but leaves
The Tuppeny hangover
The China Blackbird
The Tuppeny Bear
Cats at Christmas
I Hate Christmas

Volume 9. HIDDEN PERCEPTIONS

Silhouette on the pier
I'm not a dinosaur
Mr Mucus
The golden steps
Napoleonic Frankenstein

Volume 10. MANY CURIOUS STORIES

The house that cries
The paint brush
The man who collected smiles
Jack and the ivy
The stolen baby
The angels quest
The silly isles

Wilderness Way
I am shadow
The lift

Volume11. CHRISTMAS BOOKS 2

Christmas butterfly
The man in the library
City of laughter, city of tears
Blower Armageddon
Happy Christmas
Antman
A fairy journey
The top of the hill
The Christmas visitor
Ring up an angel
The Christmas raindrop

Volume 12.FAITH AND FAME

Fight for Faith (Gordon of Khartoum)
Angel 1818 (James Blundell)
The Saint who carried his head (St. Denis)

Volume 13. A CORNUCOPIA OF SHORT STORIES

The cursing stone
Punch and Judy (New version)
Touch of Kent dialect
One in 20 million
Be a used seed (Finding new horions)
'Open Arse' (The maligned Medlar)
Wings of colour
Elephant pin-cushion

Volume 14 **PLANTASTIC**
One in twenty million
Be a seed(Finding new horizons)
The open arse (A maligned medlar)
Nothing but leaves
Exodus to a leaf
The tulip tree
Photosynthetic women
Shepherd's purse
 The girl under the paeony tree
Jack and the ivy
Baby toes
Half a flower
How to be a successful business weed
Clingers creepers and scramblers

Volume 15 **INSECTASiA**
I am termite
Mother of hundreds
The living fossils
Human termites eat London
Brief encounters with insects
Spider in the tomb
The forlorn fruit fly
The Christmas butterfly
Towers of wax
Antman

Volume 16 **TA TA TALES**
Condiment kiss
Half a flower
Towers of wax
Gee haw whammydiddle
Peeping Tom

Flowers in the snow
One hundred
Life's escalators
Swallowed by a whale

Volume 17 Golden O0jamaflips
Mother loses leaves
Mothers of fertility
A gender fluid tree-The Mulberry
The golden chamber
The golden tongue
The little white stool
The wedding dress
I am white aphid
A letter to Lady Ellhorn
I'm coming for you now
Biscuit man
Left behind

Volume 18 WAITING TO LIGHT THE CANDLES
Take your worms to the cowshed
Baby wipe out
The blue statue
Goldrush on a banana
The Christmas taps
The three pears

Volume 19 WAVING REEDS
Pig on the roof
Greenhill school
Little miners
The Christmas baubles

Frozen frog

Volume 20 COLLECTANIA
The water poker
Shivr me timbers
The lonely wine glass
The silver mouse
The shrugger
Moby Dick in Broadstairs
The shadow man
The dancing cushions
The ear faries

OTHER STAND ALONE PUBLICATIONS at snappysnappybooks.com

Red Fred Cell and Friends (Human Biology -
advanced level
Ronnie's Sermon Snippets
Viking Bay-Natural History (Broadstairs, Kent)
The World of Wax
God rest you Merry Scrooge
Napoleonic Frankenstein
Satan's stars
HOP to Heaven
The White Lily-St Mildred-Patron Saint of Thanet
Brexit Rhymes
Earthly Quietus
I married an oak tree
The soul of the angry earthworm
Covid rhymes
Could you become a serial killer
The crocheted mouse
Keep a lamp of faith
Clowns, raibows and Christmas
Dracula's baby
Gordon of Khartoum
The Coronation of a fly

ABOUT THE AUTHOR

Dr Mike Pearce is a scientist interested in behaviour. He also was a lecturer in human biology and health at a college in Canterbury, Kent. He has written over 100 short stories as well as a many non-fiction and self-help publications

For more information see snappysnappybooks.com